~~petal~~ / ~~transport~~

~~petal~~ / ~~transport~~

James Mesiti

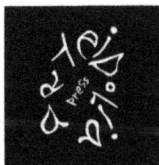

New York

ARTEIDOLIA PRESS
New York

arteidolia. com/arteidolia–press

First Edition
Library of Congress Control Number: 2024901739
ISBN: 979-8-9889702-4-8

for out there,

in here

◀ to be read ▶

becoming clay

a tongue stripped down to its ash

reader,

if you'll have me, i'd like to contradict what it means to
fade into away.

becoming clay

i.

reaching to. of reaching stairs to soil. soil to
milk jaws. this wind was broken. gravels and
fingertipped last like nothingness in god. or clear
moss that is. its row is / what was. it like to place
elbow in vessel. what branch left waters not to
continue. not to shape without door. not to know
which is to be petal and which is only. just transport.

                          best, yours.

treelands, january 13

ii.

it is getting late for lungs to theater   already. because for chloride
to stick. because to barter rounding stone.   what is strange can
be where. or cloth opens until belonging fleshes breaking. there
are no more braids here. no description / to when petal amputates
immediacy. warmth is without willingness though. warmth is.

very truly, yours.

treelands, january 16

iii.

innocence. implies untying
delicately the spider's back.
never before peeling. yet
always back into someplace.
then wait and they will bring
what hands once had to bury.
will show the needles on standby.
it means that ants are needling
again. songs of wind of ire and
stranger. forage locks of glue.
soon a clover will creep between
chests. touch heat. be tempted to
cut it out with a knife. all to
transcribe what tendon is left. all
so that someone can understand.

                    sincere apologies.

society, january 19

iv.

if heads peak to see anchor hit waist. if the opposite. if cleanse
is a trick of the rain. an idea to fix and device the falling. empty
the regime that begins at the elbow. do not. do not wrap blurred
lowlands. they will do everything they can to forgive. everything
beyond the chaos lost in gutter steam. everything not to say
home does not want to see. not to say chance won't make salt
boil over. just the rust and the animal marrow and the sea in
the shape of

    milk.]

       goodbye.

2:30am, january 26-30

4

v.

although from

bitterness. and

now and at

the hour. of

even if

from bitterness.

retiring. in the

cracks

in virginal

aisle. until

blessed be split

.be among

(be) breath´s gaze.

　　　　　　　　peace be with.

philadelphia

vi.

(after all

the hiccup still

has not clotted

no one knows

but wrapping

all the tails

in rubber bands

but he wanted

only one / she

wanted to teach

the birds how

to fall no one

knows why they

were folded

into artifice into

consciously kind

of like powder

were for

the lip

                from this rest, written to you.)

front page, february

vii.

date and deterrent and time. it will be this
epic about how gerunds cover holes at
the top then limp towards becoming clay

....

1:42am, 20th, february 3

viii.

how friction
is conjure
and accord
ingly the rain
is parallel to
what sister
said. body
in lace
of willow
you are
how /
are you

                take care.

february 5

ix.

1) part shiver-part humerus----if there is no
smoke looking to escape in glass----the surface
may not rise----may remind of once upon is
rare upon-----second preheat--next when they
wander-------tiptoe---they'll always return from
somewhere----last peel leaf by leaf--leaf by
ash and sift between------5) before tilt in the
light this light--------don't wait too soft never

positive.

february 9-12

x.

to be read aloud:
and have to reflect
psalm in a two by for-
closed was the bone
sister had seen / cried

to be read:
diverge is memory
diverge is the
memory of

to be:
collecting whisper
where artery and
page meet

                    until next.

february 13

xi.

dear – listening to   the   clouds die

must be the   most beautiful

thing. climbing   in the lack

there of   that is tendency

that is too   less   closeup is

worrying is scaffold   for what

remains of   how many   beads

until in a row   until god damn

please // although   split is the best

that can be done.   the least that can be. although

the trees are   widows

today is a widow.

....

february 16

xii.

the sky

is making a correction again. knowing where to spread

after shadow flickers – composite, shivered as the

only way the verb to partner finds a space that cannot

time to go.

12:53am, west philadelphia

xiii.

put

into   frame

a   wind

a   wind[1]

put

into   clock

february 24.

---

[1]wind in a vacuum assumes shade that of which is opposite to the body. not all can; be capable of

xiv.

IT IS NOT THAT THEY EXPECT FOR
the ear to recite just yet in the too soon
DEAD LIGHT TO BECOME
AN ANGEL DIPPED IN LITMUS

february 24.

xv.

when letters long

for incoherence

after the first

cross of the t

table that mom? dad?

that mom and dad

never made

        love but something, always.

february 24.

xvi.

an example

maybe

any   will

thread invisible

right through the

remainder then

build the end of

the hole

starting with

loose shoes for

the mud

to eat.

                                        not now.

february 27.

xvii.

knotting uneven bone will censure gravity...
compromise even when abandonment slips through hair
only then can the last leach be plucked from the moon

                  promise.

8:30am, march 1.

xviii.

sometimes brick is wander

   through a zero-sum forest

that freckles   together. that

sews apart. analogy a part

                maybe next time.

....

xix.

penance for
putting together
clavicle echo
after echo by
echo
penance for
transgressing
light to
erasure,
founding to
signifies

good luck.

fifth floor, 5:27pm, thursday

xx.

but to exist in trespass and
cadence is face value

for belonging. negotiating.
homage with rock salt

                    can't do.

12:09am, march 7, albany

xxi.

that which followed medium towards grapple.

which forecasts fencepost along sip.

which will ought and the noun forgotten.

yes, the end?

march 7

xxii.

prick specificity from wide ruled notebook line
(breathe in here, exhale)
before and almost hollow
that writes
hazard as a ghost too readied too rushed to ornament

a few moments more.

albany, ny

deserting

speech

xxiii.

before

it

barbs. doesn't it?

xxiv.

whatever is,
       whenever,
is
lingering
tentative enough
      for
the ravine to
 flatten like
missing
snow waiting-
        to
reduce with but
over
      flesh
      ------

              don't go in, not yet.

xxv.

body:
don't go in, not yet
in being puncture
from within to climb
in being absence
of perpendicular
of feather to suture
and later float

21:22, march 19

xxvi.

at last,

the temperature of falling tastes like knot about to set.

at best,

an accomplice who will sound out the axis.

xxvii.

a

letter's

fallacy

must

be

that

second

person

is

hinge

to

first,

of quoting "a few moments more"

                attentively, yours.

14:46

xxvii.

a letter's fallacy must be that second person is hinge to first, of quoting "a few moments more". a sort of umbilical twist of coming and going. a return to the scene of the template. as if a toothpick undoes itself to free up a bit of lung.

yours, attentively.

16:18

xxviii.

don't wait too   impact   planted behind

soft never   so far from a   cinder to

stray sin so   sample of   hatch / / /

close until   host held   maybe survive

                        under the lip

1995

xxix.

however, whisking silence into when makes

a dough that will rise to feel,

speak

,

and to inherit the loss of never-ripped thread

                           listening on, writing.

----

xxx.

nothing more –

for now. the water is safe to breathe. preemptively bottling

the hemistich rounds out chronology / too / comfortable

uncomfortable to strand itself in divide and in repeat.

by midnight.

march 27, 10:20am

xxxi.

Poem I:

> this poem will be
> back after the break

Sign 2:

: lapsing

into

anonymity

pores circle

their accessory

their bluff

they think

rupture,

transitive,

thinking

confection is //

therefore keep

the house

warm enough

– i will try

written and placed
4-29

xxxii.

how loss and reciprocal or bliss resign in their
consecutive?

march 27, 2023.

then, no. yes.

xxxiii.

why to explain singularity: bury. was burying? for the luck
the lack of adjective. in the hope that its carrier would place
period where farewell wouldn't. perhaps wed statement
lightly domiciled by the palm. unsure of indulgence. of the
gimmickever-enfoldedfirstpersonspilled[   ]split for agent.

                    sounds familiar.

this as from today.
                                                    .

xxxiv.

a cliché of falling through operates in wrinkle

define divine define divine vacancy. the wall is

the falling surrender. rain a toothache stirring for end.

                    stirring

stirring still.

xxxv.

on the fringes ~~of a prolific grey whose sole mention will~~,

everything that can be done has

for a hyphened rosemary politic

in denial of some, of too little monologue.

is, to yours.

6:00pm, march 30.

xxxvi.

despite

the promise

of in hiding,

promise in sharing

between and

that of double

negation. despite

composites of

welcome and

not no longer

nor nothing

more than a

contradiction

of fibers and

likenesses that

break malleable

as choice does:

as collect or

collecting voice

17:42, 82°
18:32, 81°
19:11, 78°

xxxvii.

it's _____

how the

word multiple

can constrict

in such

vulnerability

keen for

those of

whom yet to

be hidden

behind

what is to

be and

be owed

xxxviii.

across and said in another way. fault lines add immersion to

even as it seems (subtracting rare from equal likened to seam)

xxxix.

caution when defeathering the sky is manifest. is a dilute

release

of

artefact.

xl.

inventory   and

of ~~eye~~lash

malleable was

proxy recounted

and / or

correspondence

intermingling

this detour

being brought

through foreign

skip

this is how to subtitle departure.

                                   versus yours, next

april 14

xli.

contended happening

fragmented by means

and of distilling

into the sense. upstream

layering of shape.

eye~~sight~~ within

appled palm line

valid until

expires. valid

until third

person expire.

                              sign here.

follow, april 15

xlii.

twined intermediacy
branches of name

No.

ribboned, paining follicle +

unfolded absolute,

constant chew +

yearned for element,

fractal nor feel ≠

_____

anaphora being morph

      being lost above seen.

xliii.

beginning

was too

late to

preamble dirt

lightly

abbreviated

it liked to

to capture

radius whose

tongue

was the

contrary of

others.

xliv.

...never

takes

too much

to make

debris of

what is

burrowed

borrowed

and

brought

to light

by light...

xlv.

sawdust throwaways and sharpened generality to taste

=

to commit memory to memory to intervention's passing.

xlvi.

or whole but tracing return on a string. whole and heads down.
whole but enumeration of hollowed. no, of vacancy. is wholly
empty. wholly humanlike. not human, fleeting.

reader,

of worrying up until the bones that see more in the cold. more
was the urgency that unison did not try to leave. tried to imitate
repetition with aftermath. absent of membrane. absent
howevered is lost. is diluvian when wearing its noun. how the
ever so accused put this. whatever this is. altogether at last.
without but any. but any audience except for you.

- j

a tongue stripped down to its ash

shortly

and remind

that there

were those

███████

███████

███████

derived

by epigraph

███████

███████

conjugating

███████

██████ a

clearing in

the middle

of---but those

forests long

and always

pointed

to by

fracture jittering its life out of the etcetera

there may not be a more perfect day.

self-tear

self,

self-tear,

shoes,

nipple in

the shape

of the

waistline,

nerve

wrapped cork,

a tongue

stripped down

to its ash,

the am, the

momentarily

differing

brightness

engaged in

and among

afterthought,

the same

to flute index

different

to be lasting.

1) Fill in the blanks using the vocabulary words below:

starving the welcome	latitudes not longitudes	arthritis traced forward
the trope of knuckling	tangle a proximity	consonance of rust

A) Abstract spit from syllable. _____ and ransom is left.

B) Sufficiency has more to do with _____ than _____.

there is a fire happening in a place that has nothing to do with here. nothing to do with the loss of pelvic crest unless around here, arrival since there. their fresh skin and a fire so away. so not from here taking its turn hushing the pine. fired to not let metaphor takeover there. fired in the release here. yes. it is nice to hear your voice. please keep it closed keep it close. to the horns settled in velvet. to soil as it is given its graft, given at last.

winding is the wind away and passing. pass away, on.
for finally found is the tick tucked away behind the lobe.

even we.

it must have made it through the walls. snaking along the
crevasses of pink cotton candy installation, peering out of the
loose vents to come up for air. above us. suspended but not
floating. scared of what imitation floorboard and grout under
broken white tile could crackle like. it had to be the walls
because even we lock our doors most nights now. even

we acted surprised the   moment it decided to
show, astonished at   how normal it was to
listen to the ants drip   from its eyelash when
it blinked. and when it   knew that we knew it
was close. it tried not to   creep but still would
hug the plaster   avoiding the groups of
shadows that could not   join its own. it was
more relic than   heirloom. more upon

which to shed darkness. less ribs to cradle themselves as a sort
of self-defense against collapse. against all that it never asked for.
a dusted plate at the dinner table with a folding chair that could
be set out just in case. or an accomplice to help drown the salt
from the sweat ducts. it did ask for the eyes though. and knew just
when

       to

           gloss

              them

                over.

struggling to shape and take shape cloves and

their addiction to the milk chiseled away from the dawn.

to that end
where
exposure
begins and
substitutes end
is the medium
for falling

for bringing
words down
to ~~page~~ pause

words down

to where

no one will

notice no one

the mean of backfiring

draped waist equals the perimeter strangling metaphor /
besides, the gaze back-fired in rhetoric / meaning of poem: a
new word i thought i would never learn.

the purpose is to fast from certain light

(poet's note please ignore: close page, turnover assonance)

2) How can tempo antagonize ambiguity?

    a)   a translation for chaos in coherence

    b)   if upside down doesn't need a beholder

    c)   by drought

    d)   in the preterit absence must define and be defined

    e)   all of the above

    f)   none nor the above

the fiction to be. its border where

we likeness semantic and so on. on.

w ash

the salt

clears the

squirrels fatten

the snow

doesn't stick

and we

invade the

thirst and

the curtains

shutter with

night sweats

and we

wash the

bones of

their cold

and we

watch the

bones and

we watch

the cold

3) Short answer – In a paragraph of five to seven sentences describe a residency that clay will avoid. Consider the following:

- response as cause

- autonomy as effect

_____

_____

_____

_____

_____

_____

_____

_____

_____

_____

_____

_____

_____

_____

_____

_____

_____

_____

_____

_____

_____

_____

_____

let's see as

we get

closer to

fevering the

scatter

as closer

is like the

antonym

of organ

closer how

verse will lick

reference and

spit it out

by the overpass

4) True / False

for example, to mediate the light in bone

title or verse.

they arrive to what was once was. a lip is reduced to feathering. it is not the afternoon. strife is appreciated.

character 1: who to invite synonym into the whatever between crossed fingers?

character 2: you can win this time.

character 1: but it is garden in the winter.

crowd at the gate: they anti-confess! (the crowd stops knocking, holding arrest loosely)

character 2: (without concern) still there?

(a sky forgets its blanket. all search for their own gaze)

character 2: (thinks, continues) i apologize for the arcade. content craved form.

character 1: (hiding their teeth. no tongue involved) i can't be anymore.

no one at the gate: they anti-be!

(cheating reason, a new sign resumes its space)

character 3: what happened? what happened is that this is too spotted for wish.

character 2 and 3: (together with delay from one to the other) me too.

anymore

the slippage [in

sound] kept its

starving. sweat

out apostle. but

shared. the apostrophe

i didn't want. anymore.

we are not capable

of paradox. anymore.

the slippage [in

sound] maybe its

starving. sweat

out apostle. but

shared. the apostrophe

i didn't want.

circle your/the poem

interruptthewind.lostithewind.abodyinmotion.i
nterruptsthewebbing.ilostthewebbing.mechanic
unlikethehandwinding.ican'tcan'tcan'tcan'tintr
uth.intruthinmotion.intruthemotion.inplaceofthi
splace.whyweneversoughthome.interruptneithe
rbodyneithermotion.issickofunder.sufficeitsay.u
nder.enoughtosay.isitworthsheddingfor.evenifth
efishscarewhenidon'tmeanto.andthiswantstobei
ncompleteforawhile.waitingforheaventoscab.eit
herneedyorneedless.iaminthehabbitofunderstan
dingthatcontractionsleavespaceforpassivity.tool
atein.toolatetoembrace.movementsfromsoil.resi
stthefill.monopolizetheidle.thereisnoliteralbelo
nging.responsibilitywas.responsbilityis.chalkim
portingword.withpleasurewecan.circlingthesali

va on all the window joints.[2]

---

[2]consider giving to its own

trickle in

as the

foils trickle in as

bearing witness

will want to be

the answer to

nothing

indecisions. indecisions.

rubric

where few options. the shallows restart. silence squeezes itself from eyelash. where unable to story anymore or its accuracy. i wonder.

word count:

    light: 12

    bone(s): 10

    obsess: 1

the meantime

in

      this meantime witness

            will be loosely divorced

from its

appendage

i think i can finally go home.

briars. bone. this.

the briars the weeping and what is left of the
light they gave and i never knew that the
briars would sink around the stillness of
bone that weeping would seek its then heard
flesh and that this depth be as is departed.

called

i'm not talking about the appeal of the hemorrhage.

enough sentence for nothingness

to drown

and just maybe

retrace itself back to

its coal

i'm talking about this soft pain called happiness.